INUITS

JUDITH R. HARPER

SMART APPLE MEDIA MANKATO MINNESOTA

Published by Smart Apple Media
123 South Broad Street, Mankato, Minnesota 56001

Produced by The Creative Spark, San Juan Capistrano, CA
    Editor: Elizabeth Sirimarco
    Designer: Mary Francis-DeMarois
    Art Direction: Robert Court
    Page Layout: Jo Maurine Wheeler

Photos/Illustrations: Galen Rowell/Corbis 4, 26; Tessa Macintosh/ Nunavut
Tourism 6; David Hiser/Photographers/Aspen/PNI 7, 25, 27;
Kevin Davidson 8-9; Wolfgang Kaehler/Corbis 10, 20; Donna Barnett/
Nunavut Tourism 13; Lowell Georgia/Corbis pp. 16, 23; Nunavut Tourism 22

Library of Congress Cataloging-in-Publication Data
Harper, Judith E., 1953–
    Inuit / by Judith E. Harper.
      p. cm. — (Endangered cultures)
    Includes index.
    Summary: Details the history and traditional way of life of the Inuit,
the native people of the Arctic, as well as their current status and
struggle to preserve their culture and identity.
    ISBN 1-887068-74-0 (alk. paper)
    1. Inuit—History—Juvenile literature. 2. Inuit—Social life and
customs—Juvenile literature. [1. Inuit. 2. Eskimos.] I. Title. II. Series.
E99.E7H315 1999
973.04'9712—dc21   98-36409

First edition

9 8 7 6 5 4 3 2 1

Table of Contents

The Inuit have survived in the Arctic landscape of ice and snow
for thousands of years.

The World of the Inuit

The Inuit are the native people of the Arctic. They hunted and fished in this ice-covered region thousands of years before Europeans arrived. Most of the world's 125,000 Inuit inhabit the arctic and **subarctic** coastal areas of Alaska, northernmost Canada, Greenland, and northeastern Siberia.

The Arctic—the northernmost region of the world—is said to be a **circumpolar** region because the Arctic Ocean and the arctic lands surround the North Pole. This frozen, windswept world has no trees because the climate is too harsh. The flat, frozen earth is called **tundra.** Only the top few inches of soil thaw during the short, cool summers. This thawing enables some plants to grow. Tundra vegetation includes mosses, **lichen,** grasses, and low-growing shrubs, berries, and flowers. Although some thawing happens in a few places, most of the soil in the Arctic, called **permafrost,** never thaws.

Winters in the Arctic are frigid and dark, lasting at least nine months. Sub-zero temperatures chill the landscape throughout the winter. Even though ice and snow cover the entire landscape, the Arctic receives very little precipitation. Snow accumulates only because the climate

Inuit dressed in traditional clothing pick Arctic cotton, a plant hardy enough to grow during the short summers of the circumpolar region.

is too cold for it to melt most of the year. Even Summer temperatures rarely rise above 50°F (10°C).

The Inuit were nomadic hunters. Like other **nomads,** they did not settle in one place but moved their homes to find the best areas for fishing and hunting. Despite the harsh climate, wildlife such as fish, sea and land mammals, and birds abound. Today few Inuit live as nomads, but hunting remains an important part of their lives.

The ancestors of the Inuit migrated to the Arctic from Asia, arriving thousands of years after other Native American peoples came to North America from Asia. For this reason, the Inuit are more closely related to the people of Asia than to Native Americans.

The Inuit were once called Eskimos, which comes from Algonquian, a Native American language. "Eskimo" means "eaters of raw flesh" and was considered an insult. Inuit is the name the Inuit people call themselves. It means "our people" in **Inuktitut,** a common Inuit language spoken in part of Alaska, in most of Canada, and in Greenland. Other Inuit languages include Inupiaq, spoken in Northern Alaska, and Yup'ik, spoken in southwestern Alaska and Siberia. All Inuit languages are related. Speakers of one language can often understand other Inuit languages. Because of the vast area inhabited by the Inuit, there are many local **dialects.**

The ways of the Inuit vary from region to region. The Inuit of Siberia, for example, do not hunt for whales in the same way as those living in Greenland. No matter where the Inuit live, they share many beliefs and customs. For all Inuit, the Arctic environment is essential to their survival and their culture.

BEFORE 1000 A.D.

Icelanders settle in Greenland.

A hunter using a snowmobile stops for the night, building an igloo for cover. Today Inuit use modern tools to make life easier, but they still practice many of their traditional customs.

7

ARCTIC OCEAN

SIBERIA

BERING
SEA

CHUKCHI
SEA

Beluga

ST. LAWRENCE
ISLAND

BERING
STRAIT

BEAUFORT
SEA

Bowhead

NORTON SOUND

PRINCE
ALBERT SO

NUNIVAK
ISLAND

ALEUTIAN
ISLANDS

ALASKA

BRISTOL
BAY

C

KODIAK
ISLAND

PACIFIC
OCEAN

GULF OF
ALASKA

*The icy circumpolar region is the rich hunting ground of the Inuit. The game they track
includes seals, polar bears, and a variety of different whale species. This map shows the
regions where bowhead, beluga, and narwhal whales are often hunted by Inuit.*

8

NORTH
POLE

GREENLAND

ELLESMERE
ISLAND

BAY

Narwhal

BAFFIN ISLAND

ATLANTIC
OCEAN

VICTORIA
ISLAND

*FROBISHER
BAY*

KING WILLIAM
ISLAND

A D A

C A N A D A

HUDSON BAY

Snow blankets the Arctic throughout the year, so the Inuit have created many words to describe it. There are at least 20 Inuktitut words that mean snow, such as muajaq *(soft snow),* piqtuq *(blowing snow),* mingullaq *(drifted soft snow),* pukak *(first layer of snow), and* sitilluqaq *(hard snow).*

The Inuit used the kayak to hunt sea animals and to harvest fish caught in nets laid in the icy waters. Many Inuit now use boats with outboard motors instead of this traditional craft.

The Inuit Way of Life

To survive in the Arctic, the Inuit hunted. They discovered ingenious ways to hunt mammals that lived both on the land and in the sea. Everything they needed to live—food, clothing, tools, and even fuel to heat their homes—came from the animals they hunted.

The Inuit have a deep respect for animals, just as they do for the land and the oceans. They take care not to harm the environment and make sure that they do not over-hunt any one animal species. Hunters know that if they kill too many seals or **caribou** in one season, they will not be plentiful in years to come. If there is not enough game for the Inuit to hunt, their people will starve.

The Inuit believe that every living creature has a spirit. They believe they must honor the spirits of the whales, fish, and polar bears as they do the spirits of their own family members. They show respect for their prey in ceremonies they perform before, during, and after a kill. If they do not respect the spirits of the whales they hunt, the Inuit believe these mammals will leave the region forever.

In Alaska, Inuit hunt the bowhead whale; in northern Canada, the beluga whale; and in Greenland, the narwhal whale. Inuit hunters once formed large groups to hunt whales, just as they do today. Years ago, they boarded large boats called *umiaks*. These crafts had no

1500s

European explorers first land in the Arctic and meet the Inuit.

cabin to provide shelter, but waterproof walrus or seal skins covered the *umiaks*, keeping the icy sea out.

Hunters also used *kayaks*—small, flat, canoe-like boats—to hunt the beluga and the narwhal. The more experienced hunters taught the younger men and boys how to kill a whale—including how to use a harpoon, gather clues from the sea ice, and find animals in dense fog.

According to Inuit tradition, the men hunted the animals, but women have always participated. They attended the ceremonies before the hunt and sometimes joined a whale hunt to sew the *umiak* covers if they tore. After a kill, men and women butchered the dead animal. Then

THE NARWHAL

Many whales move to warmer waters during the winter, but the narwhal lives in frigid Arctic waters all year long. The narwhal is different from any other species because the male has a single, spiraled tusk that sprouts from the left side of its jaw and is usually about three feet (approximately one meter) long. Only about three percent of female narwhals have a tusk. This unusual trait gives this whale its nickname, the sea unicorn. The narwhal is seldom seen as far south as Alaska, but it is frequently hunted by the Inuit of Greenland. As of 1998, experts estimate that between 25,000 and 45,000 narwhals remain.

the women prepared the meat and **blubber** to be eaten. Although men and women performed different tasks, the Inuit say that the work of women has always been valued as much as men's work.

Just as *umiaks* and *kayaks* helped the Inuit hunt sea mammals, the dogsled helped to hunt land mammals. Caribou are plentiful throughout the North American Arctic. Like the whale, the walrus, and the seal, the caribou provide the Inuit with meat, fuel, clothing, and tools. The Inuit also hunt polar bear, wolves, foxes, **lemmings,** and **marmots,** as well as eider ducks, geese, gull, and **auk.**

1600s

European whalers and fur traders first harvest Arctic waters.

An elder Inuit teaches a young boy to use a bow and arrow. The two are dressed in animal skins to protect them from the cold that grips the circumpolar region for most of the year.

The height of European and American whaling in the Arctic.

A few Inuit still live the traditional way in outpost camps, but most families are no longer nomads, nor is hunting their way of life. Yet, many modern Inuit still need to hunt for food to supplement what they buy in stores. Instead of the dogsled, they often use snowmobiles. Instead of *umiaks* and *kayaks,* they hunt whales in boats with outboard motors. They use rifles instead of harpoons and spears. The Inuit have changed their hunting methods, but they still have the same respect for animal life as their ancestors had.

For thousands of years, the Inuit have eaten the meat and the vitamin-rich blubber of the whale, walrus, and seal. They eat fish and the meat of many land mammals and birds.

The Inuit, for the most part, prefer to live in the same community with their **extended families.** They do not all inhabit the same dwelling, however. Traditionally, and in today's world, many Inuit live in small homes with members of their immediate family. Grandparents, uncles, aunts, and cousins live nearby.

Today most Inuit live in small one-family, prefabricated houses made of wood and metal siding. When they were nomads, they built homes of sod and stone that were partly underground and were sometimes dug into a hillside. These dwellings protected the Inuit from the howling winds and cold. The igloo, a traditional shelter made of ice and snow, was often used while on hunting trips. Some Inuit in northern Greenland and Canada lived in houses of ice and snow all winter long. In the summer when they moved to hunt land mammals, they lived in caribou-skin tents. Many modern Inuit enjoy returning to a traditional way of life during the summer. They camp in canvas tents near their fishing and hunting sites.

Inuit women once made the clothing for their families. They sewed caribou skins to make warm, rugged clothing. The thread came from caribou sinews, or tendons. Their sewing needles were carved from animal bones or from the ivory tusks of walruses. Today most Inuit families buy their clothing in stores, although they may wear traditional outer clothing in the winter.

1915

The collapse of the whaling industry—whales in the Arctic are nearly extinct.

The Beluga

Belugas are small whales that reach about 15 or 16 feet (4.6 to 4.9 meters) in length. Because of their unusual white color, they are easy to distinguish from other whales. These excellent navigators can move easily through the icy waters of the Arctic. For many hundreds of years, the Canadian Inuit have hunted belugas. Today the whale's population has seriously declined because of overhunting by commercial whale hunters. Estimates suggest that only about 40,000 to 55,000 belugas now exist in Arctic waters.

15

Dead beluga whales line the shore near an Inuit whaling camp along the Beaufort Sea off Canada's Northwest Territories.

Outsiders Bring Change

At one time, the Inuit believed they were the only inhabitants of the world. Then, about 1000 years ago, people from Iceland began to settle in Greenland. European explorers sailed to Arctic shores starting in the 1500s. By the 1800s, European and American explorers, whalers, and fur traders were in frequent contact with the Inuit.

The Inuit were very interested in the newcomers' products, technology, and ideas. Metal tools and firearms entered Inuit culture. Using knives and rifles made hunting much easier.

The outsiders also created new problems for the Inuit. They brought diseases, such as influenza, smallpox, measles, and tuberculosis, killing thousands of Inuit. Whalers hunted the bowheads until they were nearly extinct. Fur trappers killed so many animals that there were not enough left for the Inuit. Without the sea and land mammals they depended on, some Inuit were left to starve.

The outsiders traded alcohol with the Inuit, who were not accustomed to alcohol and did not realize it is a substance that must be used very carefully. The use of alcohol made it more difficult for them to hunt and gather food, leaving some Inuit families to go hungry.

The Canadian government urges the Inuit to move to settlements.

In the 1950s, the government of Canada decided that it must save the Inuit. It urged them to leave their nomadic life. It offered homes to Canadian Inuit families, as well as health care, education, and money. This help was beneficial, but it did not solve all their problems.

The government has provided jobs for only a small number of Inuit. In some settlements, as many as eight out of ten adults do not have jobs. Poverty is very common. Many Inuit would not survive without the welfare money the government gives them.

Since the 1950s, nations to the south have harvested the riches of the Arctic. Private companies from the

THE BOWHEAD

Bowhead whales are named for their huge skulls, which equal about 40 percent of their total body length. These enormous whales can be anywhere from 45 to 55 feet (14 to 17 meters) long. Whalers seek out the bowhead because of its great size and the fact that the species is slow and easy to catch. Among the most seriously endangered of all whales, estimates suggest that only 8,000 bowheads remain in the world today. The Inuit of Northern Alaska still hunt this large whale according to the customs of their people, even though it has been protected by law since 1935.

United States and Canada remove oil, natural gas, and valuable minerals from the Arctic to sell in the south, taking advantage of the Arctic resources to make themselves wealthier, while the Inuit remain very poor.

The Arctic environment also has suffered from development. Tankers used to transport fuel have spilled oil into arctic and subarctic waters, causing severe ocean and coastal pollution and devastating wildlife. Construction of oil and natural gas pipelines has destroyed thousands of acres of land. **Hydroelectric** projects have caused similar damage. Although these projects have employed the Inuit, most of the jobs have been low paying and have not lasted long.

The pollution that comes from distant nations endangers both the Arctic environment and the Inuit. Pollutants enter the air and the oceans. They eventually flow into Arctic waters. These toxic chemicals have contaminated many fish and sea mammals that the Inuit depend on for food. Scientists and doctors also have found that some Inuit have been harmed by this contaminated food. **PCBs** are one pollutant that can damage the **immune system** by disrupting the function of hormones, the body's chemical messengers that tell cells, organs, and organ systems what to do. The chemicals that compose PCBs do not break down easily and accumulate in soil and water.

1971

The U.S. Congress passes the Alaska Native Claims Settlement Act, giving land back to Alaskan Inuit.

The Inuit of the Northwest Territories in Canada print road signs in both Inuktitut and English.

The Inuit Today

By the late 1960s, Inuit leaders realized they could no longer stand by and watch the destruction of the land, the oceans, their people, and their culture. They were concerned that the Inuit had to depend on outsiders to survive. They believed that if they did not take action, the Inuit people, their culture, and the Arctic environment would be lost forever.

All over the Arctic, the Inuit have joined together to save their environment and their way of life. They know that they cannot achieve their goals by working alone in their small communities. They have convinced government leaders that they need to hunt, fish, and trap animals safely and freely.

At one time, the Inuit had no choice but to live and work in isolation. Today modern communications, such as the telephone, the internet, and television (received via satellite), make it possible for them to live in a single circumpolar community. Modern air travel also knits the Arctic world together as never before.

In 1971, the Inupiat and the Yupik (Inuit groups from Alaska), as well as other Alaskan Native Americans, persuaded the United States Congress to pass the Alaska Native Claims Settlement Act. Because of this law, Alaskan natives reclaimed 44 million acres (17.7 million hectares) of their land and received nearly one billion dollars.

*The Inuit
Circumpolar
Conference (ICC)
is organized.*

*Inuit recognize the importance of teaching their children to
use computers and to speak the official language of the country
in which they live, but they also strive to teach them Inuit language,
history, and traditions.*

Since 1977, the men and women of the Inuit Circumpolar Conference (ICC) have helped the Inuit make
agreements with their national governments. As a
result, the Inuit have gained more control over how Arctic
land is used. The ICC encourages the Inuit to use the
Arctic's natural resources to earn money while preserving
the environment at the same time.

In 1982, the Inuit Broadcasting Corporation (IBC)
began presenting television programs to the Inuit of
Canada. Inuit leaders have long been concerned about
the television programs that come from the United
States and southern Canada, believing that these shows
may keep the Inuit from preserving their own culture.
Consequently, IBC programs educate the Inuit about

their traditions, art, and literature. *Takuginai* (which means "Look Here" in Inuktitut) is an IBC children's show that is much like *Sesame Street*. Arctic animal characters, like Johnny the Lemming, teach children about the Inuktitut language and Inuit culture.

1977

The Trans-Alaska Pipeline is completed.

Scientists conduct controlled oil spills on Arctic ice to monitor damage and to see how quickly the oil travels. Oil spills have endangered many Arctic animals.

1982

The Inuit Broadcasting Corporation (IBC) begins to broadcast Inuit programming.

In Canada, Inuit leaders have worked for more than 25 years to gain control of native lands. Finally, in 1993, the Canadian government signed an agreement to create a new territory. Nunavut, which means "our land" in Inuktitut, became an official Canadian territory in 1999. This enormous land was formerly part of the Northwest Territory and is now governed by Inuit leaders. The Inuit of Canada will be able to make decisions to protect their land, their people, and their way of life.

Mary Simon, an **Inuk,** was appointed Canada's first ambassador of the Arctic. She and other Inuit leaders are working to make global trade a reality. She believes that the Inuit can become stronger and more independent if they sell their meat, fur, and animal-skin products

WHALES AND THE ENVIRONMENT

Scientists know the Arctic environment is undergoing drastic changes. The Earth is becoming warmer, and climate changes make survival difficult for marine life adapted to the frosty Arctic waters. Toxic pollution also continues to damage the ocean and its inhabitants. Inuit have known for many years that overharvesting by commercial whalers has seriously endangered the whale populations they rely on for food and energy. Now there is a new concern: Whale meat may not even be safe to eat.

The Exxon Valdez oil tanker runs aground in southern Alaska. Ten million gallons of oil damage the ocean, the coastline, and millions of animals.

The world of the Inuit is filled with traditions from their past, but also with modern conveniences. A hunter uses a dogsled to help hunt land mammals. Behind him is a satellite dish that carries television signals to the isolated Arctic from far away.

The Canadian government signs an agreement to make Nunavut an Inuit territory of Canada by 1999.

A scientist with the Environmental Protection Agency checks Alaskan waters for contamination.

on the world market. If the Inuit are strong, she says, they will be better able to face the problems that the 21st century will bring to the Arctic.

Simon is also a top leader of the Arctic Council, a group of Inuit and non-Inuit leaders and scientists from eight nations. The Arctic Council works with the Inuit Circumpolar Conference and the United Nations to protect the Arctic and its inhabitants, trying to persuade world leaders to reduce ocean pollution.

The Arctic Council is urging other nations to take steps to reduce **global warming**. No one knows for sure if it is the burning of **fossil fuels** that is causing the earth to become warmer. Whatever the reason, the Arctic climate is heating up. The Inuit know they need to be prepared if the frozen land they depend on continues to change.

The Inuit are hopeful about their future. They believe they will solve their problems and keep their culture alive so that their children will inherit a land where they can live healthy, independent lives in harmony with the environment.

1996

The Arctic Council is formed to protect the Arctic and its inhabitants.

The Inuit plan to keep their unique culture alive, even as the world around them changes.

Glossary

auk
Diving seabirds that the Inuit hunt for food.

blubber
The fat of whales and other large sea mammals used by the Inuit both as food and as fuel to warm and light their houses.

caribou
Large deer that live in herds in northern North America and are often hunted by Inuit.

circumpolar
Located in or near a polar region, literally "around the pole."

dialects
Regional differences in a language, such as variations in vocabulary, pronunciation, and sentence structure.

extended families
Family units made up of not only parents and children, but grandparents, aunts, uncles, and cousins as well.

fossil fuels
Petroleum products (including fuel oil and gasoline), coal, and natural gas.

global warming
An increase in the earth's average temperature. Some scientists believe global warming is caused by the burning of fossil fuels.

hydroelectric
Using water power to make electricity.

immune system	The parts of the body that fight infection and prevent disease.
Inuk	An Inuit person.
Inuktitut	The language spoken by the Inuit in northern Alaska, Canada, and Greenland.
kayaks	Small, canoe-like boats.
lemmings	Small, furry rodents of the arctic and subarctic regions.
lichen	A plant consisting of fungi and algae, often found growing on rocks and trees.
marmots	Large, full-bodied, furry rodents; a woodchuck or groundhog is a type of marmot.
nomads	People who travel from place to place and do not have a fixed home.
PCBs	Toxic chemical substances (polychlorinated biphenyls) used in the manufacture of a variety of products, including electrical equipment, plastics, and building materials.

permafrost   The permanently frozen soil beneath the surface of the ground in Arctic regions.

subarctic   South of the Arctic.

tundra   The frozen, treeless land of the Arctic.

umiaks   Large, open boats covered with seal or walrus skins and used for whale hunting.

Further Reading and Information

BOOKS AND MAGAZINE ARTICLES:

Fleischner, Jennifer. *The Inuit: People of the Arctic*. Millbrook, CT: Millbrook Press, 1995.

Hancock, Lyn. *Nunavut*. Minneapolis, MN: Lerner Publications, 1995.

Meyer, Carolyn. *In a Different Light: Growing Up in a Yupik Eskimo Village in Alaska*. New York, NY: Simon & Schuster, 1996.

People of the Ice and Snow. Alexandria, VA: Time-Life Books, 1994.

"Peoples of the Arctic." *National Geographic*, February, 1983

WEB SITES:

The Inuit Circumpolar Conference web site has a variety of information about the Inuit: http://www.inusiaat.com

Index

Items in bold print indicate illustration.